D0604759

GHANA

...in Pictures

Visual Geography Series®

GHANA

...in Pictures

Prepared by
Geography Department

Lerner Publications Company
Minneapolis

Independent Picture Service

**Timber is sorted and graded in Kumase before being
shipped by rail to Sekondi-Takoradi for export.**

This is an all-new edition of the Visual Geography
Series. Previous editions have been published by
Sterling Publishing Company, New York City, and
some of the original textual information has been re-
tained. New photographs, maps, charts, captions, and
updated information have been added. The text has
been entirely reset in 10/12 Century Textbook.

LIBRARY OF CONGRESS CATALOGING-IN-PUBLICATION DATA

Ghana in pictures.

(Visual geography series)
Rev. ed. of: Ghana in pictures / prepared by Lýdia
Verona Zemba.
Includes index.
Summary: Describes the history, geography, government, economy, culture, and people of the African country once known as the Gold Coast.
1. Ghana. [1. Ghana] I. Zemba, Lýdia Verona. Ghana
in pictures. II. Lerner Publications Company. Geography Dept. III. Series: Visual geography series (Minneapolis, Minn.)
DT510.G46   1988   966.7'.05   87-17260
ISBN 0-8225-1829-5 (lib. bdg.)

International Standard Book Number: 0-8225-1829-5
Library of Congress Catalog Card Number: 87-17260

VISUAL GEOGRAPHY SERIES®

Publisher
Harry Jonas Lerner
Associate Publisher
Nancy M. Campbell
Senior Editor
Mary M. Rodgers
Editor
Gretchen Bratvold
Illustrations Editor
Karen A. Sirvaitis
Consultants/Contributors
Thomas O'Toole
Sandra K. Davis
Designer
Jim Simondet
Cartographer
Carol F. Barrett
Indexer
Sylvia Timian
Production Manager
Richard J. Hannah

Independent Picture Service

**Almost 50 percent of Ghana's population is under the age
of 15.**

Acknowledgments

Title page photo courtesy of World Bank.

Elevation contours adapted from *The Times Atlas of
the World*, seventh comprehensive edition (New York:
Times Books, 1985).

2 3 4 5 6 7 8 9 10 97 96 95 94 93 92 91 90 89

Fishermen at Elmina, Ghana's second largest port after Tema, work from traditional canoes. Many fishermen also use modern motorized boats.

Contents

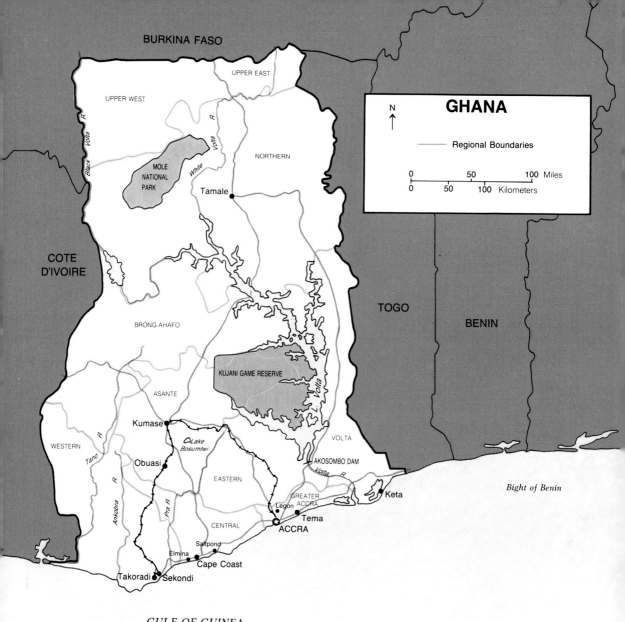

BURKINA FASO

UPPER EAST

UPPER WEST

COTE
D'IVOIRE

Black Volta R.

Volta R.

MOLE
NATIONAL
PARK

White Volta

NORTHERN

Tamale

TOGO

BENIN

BRONG-AHAFO

KUJANI GAME RESERVE

L. Volta

ASANTE

Kumase

Tano R.

WESTERN

OLake
Bosumtwi

Obuasi

Ankobra R.

Pra R.

EASTERN

VOLTA

AKOSOMBO DAM

Volta R.

Keta

Bight of Benin

CENTRAL

GREATER
ACCRA

Legon

Tema

ACCRA

Saltpond

Elmina

Cape Coast

Takoradi

Sekondi

GULF OF GUINEA

GHANA

N

— Regional Boundaries

| 0 | 50 | 100 Miles |
| 0 | 50 | 100 Kilometers |

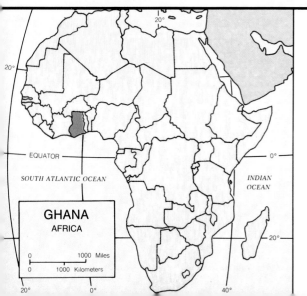

20°

20°

20°

EQUATOR

0°

SOUTH ATLANTIC OCEAN

INDIAN
OCEAN

20°

GHANA
AFRICA

| 0 | 1000 Miles |
| 0 | 1000 Kilometers |

20°   0°   40°

METRIC CONVERSION CHART
To Find Approximate Equivalents

WHEN YOU KNOW:	MULTIPLY BY:	TO FIND:
AREA		
acres	0.41	hectares
square miles	2.59	square kilometers
CAPACITY		
gallons	3.79	liters
LENGTH		
feet	30.48	centimeters
yards	0.91	meters
miles	1.61	kilometers
MASS (weight)		
pounds	0.45	kilograms
tons	0.91	metric tons
VOLUME		
cubic yards	0.77	cubic meters
TEMPERATURE		
degrees Fahrenheit	0.56 (*after* subtracting 32)	degrees Celsius

Ghana's rich, colorful *kente* cloth is handwoven, using a technique that is over 250 years old.

Introduction

Since gaining independence from Great Britain in 1957, the Republic of Ghana—formerly known as the Gold Coast—has become one of the best known of Africa's 51 countries. Ghana's first national leader, Kwame Nkrumah, is remembered throughout the world. He enabled members of his Convention People's party (CPP) to resist British colonial policies peacefully yet effectively. In its early years, Ghana was regarded as a shining example among emerging nations and as a model of orderly resistance to economic dependence on foreign powers.

In the 1980s, however, Ghana faces pressing national problems. Since independence, Ghana's government has changed eight times, and military coups d'état have become commonplace. The 1988 government has not developed a consistent policy to meet the country's needs, and social unrest and civilian disorders are widespread. The great political promise of the 1950s and 1960s has given way to curfews,

The symbol of the Asante people—one of the largest ethnic groups in Ghana—is the golden stool, which represents group solidarity.

closed borders, and government control of the press.

Moreover, since gaining independence in 1957, Ghana's economy has declined at an alarming rate. Food resources are inadequate and unemployment is high. The low price of Ghana's major export—cacao (the raw material of chocolate)—and the rising cost of imports contribute to the worsening of economic conditions. Meanwhile, the price of food is skyrocketing.

How did Ghana—once a strong and wealthy West African nation—become entangled in such threatening political and economic problems? Part of the answer lies in a complex history of unstable governments and natural disasters. How Ghanaians will reverse three decades of economic decline—and move again toward strength and prosperity—is a question of global concern.

The next generation of Ghanaians faces the challenges of worsening economic conditions and an unstable government.

Behind the dam at Akosombo lies Lake Volta, the largest artificial lake in the world, covering over 3,000 square miles.

1) The Land

The modern nation of Ghana consists of four regions—the former British colony called the Gold Coast, the Asante region, the Northern Territories, and British Togoland. The country has an area of 92,100 square miles—slightly smaller than the state of Oregon. Situated in West Africa with its southern shore on the Gulf of Guinea, Ghana—an almost rectangular country—is bordered on the west by Côte d'Ivoire, on the northwest and north by Burkina Faso (formerly Upper Volta), and on the east by Togo.

Topography

Except for the Akuapem-Togo Range on its eastern frontier, Ghana is characterized by low, fertile plains and scrubland, which are separated by several rivers and by Lake Volta. Half of the country lies less than 500 feet above sea level. Its highest point—Mount Afadjoto, located in the southeastern hills—reaches to only 2,905 feet in height. The land includes three main regions: the southern coastal area, the southwestern forest belt, and the northern dry savanna.

Courtesy of Mary Gemignani
Courtesy of Mary Gemignani

Ghana has more than 300 miles of low, sandy shore stretching along the waters of the Gulf of Guinea.

Courtesy of Helaine K. Minkus

Banana plants grow in the dense rain-forests of the western inland region.

The coastline of Ghana consists mostly of a low, sandy shore with occasional high, rocky masses. Although no natural harbors exist, many curving beaches line the shore. On the eastern end of the coast near the mouth of the Volta River, lagoons and sandbars are found. Just behind the central and eastern shoreline, low-lying plains —with short grasses, dense shrubs, and scattered trees—stretch for about 60 miles inland.

Ghana's forest belt—also known as the Asante region—extends in an L-shape over the southwestern interior. Most of the country's cacao, minerals, and timber come from the rich soil of this heavily forested area. True rain-forest—with dense groves of trees, some towering to heights of 200 feet—is found in the extreme southwestern corner of the forest belt. Here annual rainfall ranges from 65 to 86 inches, and humidity is very high, often reaching 100 percent.

Although parts of Ghana's forest region are cleared periodically for farming operations, forest reserves claim much of the area. The reserves slow the harvest of timber and protect the headwaters of streams that run through the area. The forests also break the force of the harmattan—a dry, dust-laden wind that blows down from the Sahara Desert.

North of the great forests, Ghana's land gradually becomes drier. The gently rolling savanna—stretching over a vast area of 65,000 square miles—includes grassy plains, low bushes, widely spaced trees, and occasional swampland. While most of the northern grasses are short, some reach a height of 12 feet.

The savanna country lies in a zone with a desertlike dry season. From late November to mid-March, when the harmattan blows severely and humidity is low, the northern soil becomes baked and cracked, and the grasses and trees turn yellow. Many trees in this region are fire-resistant, having developed thick barks that can withstand strong winds and long droughts.

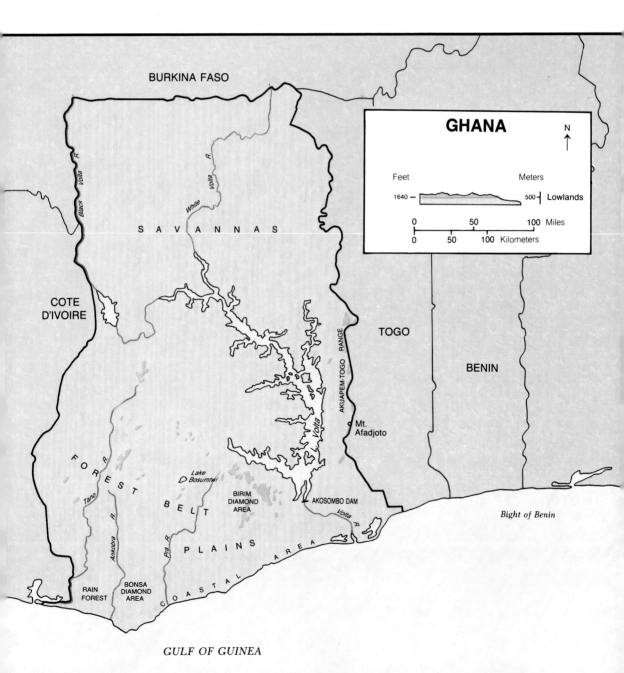

GULF OF GUINEA

Waterways

Ghana's many waterways include a large number of streams and rivers. In addition, several coastal lagoons, a large lake, and a vast artificial reservoir dot the land.

Although the close network of waterways covers most of the country, few rivers and streams maintain an even flow throughout the year. Because they are fed primarily by springs and by the rainfall of the wet season, many waterways in Ghana shrink or dry up completely during the height of the dry season. Traffic on Ghana's streams and rivers thus depends on the time of year, and, during much of the year, only lightweight craft such as canoes can navigate the shallow waters.

Until recently, the country's land drainage was dominated by the Volta River. The Volta's main incoming branches, the White Volta and the Black Volta, enter Ghana from Burkina Faso and Côte d'Ivoire, respectively. The completion of the Akosombo Dam in southeastern Ghana in 1966 transformed the Volta River system into the world's largest artificial lake. Forming a spectacular feature of Ghana's geography, this massive reservoir of water —called Lake Volta—covers about 3,500 square miles and extends to over 300 miles in length.

West of the Volta, several smaller rivers, such as the Pra, the Ankobra, and the Tano reach the sea. Lake Bosumtwi lies in Ghana's south central interior. With banks rising from 500 to 1,400 feet, the large lake is spectacularly beautiful.

Climate

Although located in the tropics just above the equator, Ghana has moderate temperatures, constant breezes, and clear sunshine most of the year. Generally, southern

The largest river in Ghana is the Volta, which begins in a branch called the White Volta in Burkina Faso, a country located south of the Sahara Desert.

Independent Picture Service

The highest elevations in Ghana are found in the southeastern hills near the nation's border with Togo.

temperatures range from 75° F in October to 85° F in June. The eastern coast is warm and somewhat dry, while the southwest corner is hot and humid.

Farther north, in Ghana's savanna country, climatic conditions are more extreme. The dry season that exists in this region from November to March includes daytime temperatures that reach 100° F, low humidity, high winds, and severe dust storms—all consequences of the harmattan. During this dry period, parched air draws moisture from the vegetation, and many trees lose their leaves. Although the entire country experiences the dry season to some extent, the coastal area feels it for only two or three weeks because sea breezes help to reduce temperatures.

Like other countries in the tropics, Ghana receives a considerable amount of rainfall. Average annual totals range from 86 inches in the southwest to 29 inches in the southeast. The coastal plain and the forest area have two rainy seasons—the long rains, which pour down from April to July, and the short rains, which last from September to November. In the north, however, there is only one rainy season, from April to September.

Courtesy of Embassy of Ghana

Trees in Ghana's dense tropical forests receive ample rainfall during two annual rainy seasons and may grow to heights of 200 feet.

13

A wide variety of lush grasses, bushes, plants, and trees flourishes in Ghana.

Flora and Fauna

The overall number of plants and animals in Ghana has declined somewhat, especially in the northeastern part of the country, because of the clearing of land for agricultural use. Valuable hardwoods—such as African mahogany, obeche, and sapele—continue to flourish, however. Giant silk-cotton trees and cedars remain plentiful in the tropical forest of the south. Oil palms grow in the south, while in the north hardy baobabs, shea trees, and several types of fine-leafed acacia are found.

A variety of herbs, scrub, low bushes, and grasses—especially guinea grass—thrive in southern Ghana. Although not native to Ghana, cacao trees—important to the world's production of chocolate—now cover some 4.5 million acres of land in the south and west. Throughout the extensive savanna in the central and northern areas, densely matted tussock grasses and occasional broad-leaved trees are found. Mole National Park is located in the northern region just west of the White Volta River.

Ghana's animal life includes buffalo, leopards, porcupines, wild hogs, antelope, hyenas, and monkeys. Rodents and lizards abound. Many species of snakes—cobras, pythons, puff adders, and horned adders—can be found in Ghana's lowlands, swamps, and dense tropical forests. Crocodiles and hippopotamuses sun themselves on the river banks. Just west of the widest portion of Lake Volta is the Kujani Game Reserve.

Over 300 species of birds have been reported in Ghana, including swallows, parrots, herons, eagles, and vultures. Goats, sheep, cattle, and chickens—each numbering in the millions—make up a large part of Ghana's domestic animal population. In the deep sea, tuna, herring, and bream are plentiful, while sardines and mackerel live in Ghana's inland waters.

Courtesy of Stephen Mustoe

The cattle egret, native to almost all of Africa, is among 300 species of birds in Ghana.

Crocodiles sun themselves on river banks with their mouths open—revealing dozens of teeth.

Accra, with a population of 958,000, is the capital and administrative center of Ghana and the country's largest city. A combination of new and old architectural styles and lush greenery characterize the city. The streets of Accra are alive with cars, trucks, buses, street vendors, and domestic animals.

Courtesy of Embassy of Ghana

Accra

Accra, a port located on the eastern coast, is Ghana's capital and largest city. Originally a small fishing village, Accra became the capital of the Gold Coast in 1877. Perhaps because of its 300-year history of contact with the European world, Accra was the first city in Ghana to develop foreign business offices, hospitals, and schools. Luxury items from other countries arrived at Accra's docksides before being delivered to other colonial towns.

Modern Accra—with a population of almost one million people—is the key city for all of the nation's governmental and business activities. Major roads, airlines, railways, buses, and ocean liners serve the capital, connecting it to most other large cities of southern Ghana.

Merging with several other coastal towns, Accra has developed into the Accra-Tema area, forming the country's chief commercial, industrial, and transportation center. The population of this fast-growing metropolitan region, now called Greater Accra, reached 1.5 million in 1984. Modern Tema—at the far eastern end of this urban sprawl, just 30 miles from Accra—has huge factories and well-planned housing areas.

Most major public ceremonies are staged in Black Star Square in Accra, which is also a popular tourist attraction.

Kumase—a thriving commercial and cultural center—is located in Ghana's Asante country in the south central interior.

Secondary Cities

With a population of more than 350,000, Kumase is the commercial, cultural, and educational hub of the Ghanaian interior. Headquarters of the wealthy Asante region since the seventeenth century, Kumase lies inland about 200 miles northwest of Accra. A hilly city with beautiful, wooded valleys, Kumase was known at one time as the "Garden City" and the "City of the Golden Stool."

Connected by rail and road with Accra and Takoradi, Kumase serves as the market town for the surrounding cacao- and timber-producing regions. In addition, heavy trade in minerals—especially gold—flourishes in and around Kumase.

Tamale, with about 220,000 people, is the administrative capital of Ghana's Northern Region. Products such as rice, cotton, butter, and peanuts are shipped out of the north by way of Tamale.

The coastal towns of Sekondi-Takoradi, Cape Coast, Elmina, Saltpond, and Keta—where the Europeans first established trading posts—are located along the Gulf of Guinea. Two port cities, Sekondi-Takoradi and Tema, have artificial harbors to handle the tons of cargo that enter and leave Ghana every year.

Photo by Eliot Elisofon, Eliot Elisofon Archives, National Museum of African Art, Smithsonian Institution

Elmina, one of the oldest European settlements in Ghana, lies on the Gulf of Guinea west of Accra.

Photo by Phil Porter

Now a prison, Cape Coast Castle was completed by the British in 1662. Europeans erected many forts along the Ghanaian coast beginning in the fifteenth century.

2) History and Government

Over a period of 2,000 years, farming peoples slowly moved into the forest regions of West Africa. Gradually they absorbed and displaced the hunting and gathering peoples that originally had lived there. By carving out villages in the forests, the farmers established agricultural settlements to grow yams, bananas, and other forest-adapted crops.

In the Sudan—a great, treeless plain stretching across northern Africa from the Atlantic Ocean to the Red Sea—large, well-organized states were established in about the fourth century A.D. An active, trans-Saharan caravan trade—in gold, slaves, horses, woven goods, and salt—played a vital role in Ghana's development as a nation. The caravans also spread ideas, education, and religious thought. At the height of their power, these African states were empires, covering vast areas and governing neighboring peoples. Three of the most notable empires—Ghana, Mali, and Songhai—stand out in history.

19

The ancient empires of Ghana and Mali were celebrated for their wealth of gold. Intricately carved weights made of the precious metal were often used to measure gold dust in trading.

The Ghana Empire

The boundaries of the ancient empire of Ghana—from which the modern nation took its name—existed several hundred miles north of the border of the modern republic. Nevertheless, present-day Ghanaians look to the Ghana Empire as the source of their cultural history.

The exact origins of the ancient empire remain unclear, but it existed as early as the beginning of the eighth century and reached the height of its prosperity and strength by the tenth century. Formed by a Soninke community that had migrated from the Sudan region, the Ghana Empire evolved into a highly advanced civilization. While the empire included many Muslims—followers of the Islamic religion—it was primarily a state that embraced traditional African religious beliefs.

The Ghana Empire gradually came to control the entire southwestern section of the trans-Saharan trade route—governing, in particular, the gold-producing region. Despite its economic prosperity, however, the empire began to collapse when attacked by a warring group of Muslim reformers called the Almoravids.

The Almoravids captured Ghana in 1076, and many of the Soninke were massacred or forced to accept Islam. The Ghana Empire weakened further, and the trans-Saharan trade—so essential to the state's economic well-being—was severely disrupted. By the thirteenth century, the empire had been destroyed.

The Mali Empire

From the ruins of the Ghana Empire arose the empire of Mali. Like Ghana, it was noted for its golden treasures. Three great kings—Sundiata, Mansa Uli, and Mansa Musa—expanded Mali until it became one of the greatest empires of the fourteenth century.

As a Muslim state, Mali developed major cultural centers and reached its peak under the leadership of the emperor Mansa

The Mali and Songhai empires established the Islamic religion in Ghana and developed important centers of learning and culture. The greatest ruler of the Songhai Empire, Askia Muhammad, was a devout Muslim, or follower of Islam.

Musa. He soon became well known for his justice, love of learning, and wealth. His showy pilgrimage to Mecca by way of Cairo in 1324 attracted attention to Mali. Many traders and scholars, learning of the empire's great wealth and of its educational and cultural achievements, came to Mali to live and work.

With the establishment of a mosque (Islamic holy place) and learning center at Tombouctou and continued economic development, the fame of the Mali Empire spread to the far corners of the known world. Like other Sudanic kingdoms, however, Mali rested on weak foundations that provided no orderly system for choosing leaders. By the end of the fourteenth century, Mali's golden age had passed. By the mid-fifteenth century Mali was overcome by the Songhai Empire.

The Songhai Empire

The Songhai people, originally a small agricultural and fishing community, were first located in the middle regions along the Niger River. After moving farther upstream to Gao, the Songhai were better able to trade with the north and soon overpowered the weakening Mali Empire.

The Songhai Empire was at the height of its power by the mid-sixteenth century. Its greatest ruler was Askia Muhammad, known as Askia the Great. A devout Muslim, Askia Muhammad worked to establish the Islamic code of law in the Sudan. He gave Muslim scholars special status by granting them lands, and, under his patronage, Tombouctou flourished as an unrivaled center of learning. The innovative ruler divided the government into administrative, economic, and military units and the empire itself into provinces.

In spite of his many achievements and progressive measures, however, Askia Muhammad was dethroned in 1528 by his three sons, who had shared power with him. Over the next several years, the Songhai Empire decayed politically. In 1591, at the Battle of Tondibi, invading Moors from North Africa inflicted a crushing defeat on the Songhai.

The 200-year-old Larabanga Mosque (Muslim place of worship) in northern Ghana displays a unique architectural design. Although Islam was established in Ghana several centuries ago, today only about 12 percent of the population are Muslims.

Courtesy of Embassy of Ghana

Migrations to Present-Day Ghana

Some modern Ghanaians claim that they are descended from ancient West African empires and kingdoms. But it is more commonly believed that a series of immigrations brought together the ancestors of present-day Ghanaians. Beginning in the fifteenth century, Ga-Adangme and Ewe peoples—who are related to the Yoruba and Fon groups of present-day Nigeria and Benin—emigrated from the east. By 1660 a community called Accra was on its way to becoming the capital of the Ga federation, whose settled area extended throughout the southeastern coastal plain and the Volta River Basin.

Meanwhile, the founding rulers of the savanna kingdoms of Dagomba and Mamprussi began arriving from the north. In some areas they displaced the original Gur- and Kwa-speaking peoples; in others, they simply imposed their leadership on already established communities. Later, in the seventeenth century, Mande-speaking peoples from present-day Mali took over Akan villages located between the Dagomba kingdom and the western forest belt. These peoples settled and established the state of Gonja.

Despite these waves of immigrants, local inhabitants lived in relatively isolated communities until the late eighteenth century. At that time clusters of villages

Independent Picture Service

A wood carving shows an umbrella—a traditional symbol of leadership—above an Asante ruler, the Queen Mother, and several attendants.

began to band together under one ruler. The most highly organized and militaristic of these clusters were the Asante, or Akan people, of the south central interior.

Trade with Europeans

Although fairly frequent contact between Europe and North Africa had occurred for many centuries, most of the West African coast remained outside of Europe's commercial routes until the fifteenth century.

Independent Picture Service

Ghana's early history can be seen in the line of forts constructed by Europeans along the Gold Coast. Ownership of the forts changed hands for several centuries as European powers tried to control trade in the region. The two forts shown in this eighteenth-century print still stand in Accra.

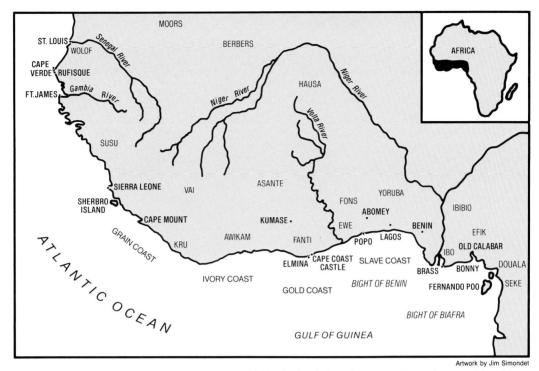

MOORS

ST. LOUIS
WOLOF
BERBERS
CAPE VERDE RUFISQUE
Senegal River
HAUSA
FT. JAMES *Gambia River*
Niger River
Niger River
AFRICA

SUSU
Volta River

SIERRA LEONE VAI ASANTE YORUBA
SHERBRO ISLAND FONS ABOMEY IBIBIO
CAPE MOUNT KUMASE • EWE BENIN EFIK
GRAIN COAST KRU AWIKAM FANTI POPO LAGOS OLD CALABAR
ELMINA CAPE COAST CASTLE SLAVE COAST IBO BRASS BONNY DOUALA
IVORY COAST FERNANDO POO SEKE
GOLD COAST *BIGHT OF BENIN*
BIGHT OF BIAFRA
A T L A N T I C   O C E A N
GULF OF GUINEA

Artwork by Jim Simondet

European traders gave names to the western coast of Africa in the eighteenth century. The various coastal regions—Grain Coast, Ivory Coast, Gold Coast (now Ghana)—referred to the principal commodities available in these areas. The Bights (bays) of Benin and Biafra were familiar landmarks to slave traders navigating the coast. Names of local peoples who lived in West Africa are shown on the map in light type.

Closed trade routes to Asia made it necessary for Europe to find new ways to reach the splendid markets of the Orient. As a result, the Portuguese explored the West African coast in the early 1400s and led the way for traders from other European countries.

By the middle of the fifteenth century, the Portuguese had begun to trade with peoples they encountered on the West African coast. The large profits gained by the Portuguese—mainly in gold dust—led them to name the coastal territory the Gold Coast. Wishing to establish a well-defined and fortified trading center as well as to safeguard their monopoly over the riches of this region, the Portuguese negotiated with the local leader at Elmina for permission to build a stronghold. Thus, after gaining a lease of land in 1482, they built San Jorge Castle—a fortress now known as Elmina Castle.

The Portuguese continued their profitable trading on the Gold Coast until the mid-seventeenth century. In 1637, the Dutch captured Elmina Castle, and by 1642 the Portuguese had been driven out. For a brief time, the Dutch and British maintained strong control over the coastal trade.

Gold Coast profits soon attracted adventurers and merchants from several other European countries, and a spirited rivalry developed among the many competing European interests—each wanting to keep the trade for itself. Between 1482 and 1800 at least 40 forts and castles were built along the Gold Coast as various European nations—Britain, Holland, Portugal, Sweden, Denmark, and Germany—attempted

Portuguese explorers, attracted by gold, were the first Europeans to land in Ghana. In 1482 they established a trading settlement at Elmina and built an important stronghold there *(above)*.

to protect their holdings. By the mid-eighteenth century, competition for the jealously guarded gold markets occurred up and down the west coast.

As European traders engaged in bitter struggles with one another, ownership of the forts often changed hands. Occasionally the forts were surrounded and taken over by local peoples.

The Slave Trade

Originally the Europeans came to West Africa to trade in gold, ivory, and pepper. But the founding of settlements in the Americas and the establishment there of sugar, tobacco, and cotton plantations caused a great demand for a regular sup-

ply of laborers. Consequently, an extensive slave trade developed, centered along the Guinea coast of West Africa. Ships brought goods from Europe to sell on the West African coast, took slaves across the Atlantic for sale in the Americas, and finally returned to Europe loaded with New World sugar, tobacco, and cotton.

From the mid-1600s until the late 1700s, the Gold Coast contributed about 10,000 slaves each year to the Atlantic slave trade. At that time this amount was a large percentage of the total number of Africans being shipped to the New World. Later, as the volume of the trade grew, the Gold Coast contributed fewer slaves in proportion to the number exported from present-day Benin and Nigeria.

Britain's economic and political domination of the Gold Coast was a direct result of slave trade competitions with other European nations—especially with the Dutch—in the seventeenth and eighteenth centuries. The British Royal African Company, having established 10 forts along the Gold Coast by 1700, soon effectively rivaled the Dutch West India Company.

The business was also profitable for some African groups, who captured and sold the slaves to European slave traders. At the turn of the eighteenth century, the Asante—who had emerged as the dominant African power in the western interior of the Gold Coast—controlled that area's market in gold, ivory, and slaves. The Asante leaders ran a regional trading operation, and they often used force to open routes leading to the coast.

Trade wars kept the region in turmoil, and the African coastal states sometimes participated in the struggles. In 1694, for example, the Dutch persuaded the Asante to attack the British fort at Sekondi on the Gulf of Guinea.

Courtesy of Library of Congress

After the discovery of the New World, which created an immense demand for labor, the Gold Coast became active in the slave trade. From the mid-1600s until the mid-1800s, the Gold Coast contributed thousands of slaves each year. They were shipped to the West Indies and the Americas, where they were exchanged for minerals and food to be sold in Europe.

Transactions between European trading companies and African merchants at the local markets, however, soon became well organized. The slaves that were captured to be sold at the markets were often prisoners acquired through local conflicts, such as border disputes. Africans rarely offered their relatives into slavery. More frequently, servants, criminals, debtors, drifters, and refugees were bound and sold.

Because of the regularity of the slave trade, terms for buying and selling became almost routine. European goods and African slaves were valued according to standard units of gold dust on the Gold Coast. The goods most desired by the African traders were guns and gunpowder, cloth, alcohol, tobacco, and hardware. Local rulers, in order to acquire more exotic or expensive goods, sometimes demanded additional fees.

Effects of the Trade

The introduction of foreign goods to the Gold Coast had some far-reaching effects. The unusually rapid development of the Asante people into a large and powerful empire, for instance, was directly related to their acquisition of muskets and gunpowder through the Atlantic trade. Although imported firearms served to strengthen Africans against European invasion, access to large quantities of weapons also fostered war among Africans. In many cases, when African kings and elders saw how destructive this trade had become to the peace and prosperity of their realms, they tried hard to bring it to a halt.

Other imports significant to the Gold Coast were new food plants—especially cassava (an edible root), maize (corn), and sweet potato—brought by the Portuguese from the tropics of South America. These new food supplies flourished in the humid regions of the Gold Coast and helped to feed repopulated areas where great numbers had been lost to the slave trade.

The Nineteenth Century

British influence along the coast of present-day Ghana grew rapidly after 1800. Traders began working with local peoples living around the long-established, British-held forts. The Asante leaders of the interior and the British merchants did not wish to stop the still-profitable slave trade, which the British government was attempting to end. Although the Atlantic slave trade was officially abolished by Britain in 1807, the actual practice ended only gradually—indeed, some slave trade continued until about 1850.

Meanwhile, European and North American missionaries began to arrive in the territory to preach their religion as well as

African traders sometimes used brass weights to measure gold dust when bartering with early European colonists.

Courtesy of Dr. Deborah Pellow

A woman stirs corn porridge made from maize, a staple crop originally introduced to Ghana by the Portuguese.

Independent Picture Service

European and North American missionaries began to arrive in Ghana in the mid-nineteenth century. Their influence—represented by these Anglican churchgoers in Accra—is still noticeable.

to work in education, health training, child welfare, and the scientific cultivation of food. The Presbyterian Basel Mission of 1828 went to the eastern Accra region, and the Bremen Mission of 1847 gained a firm footing in the Volta region. Later, in 1875, the Methodist Church was established at Cape Coast.

The missionaries introduced crops for export, new industries, and Western occupations. They built and staffed schools, hospitals, and clinics. Many studied the local languages and put them into written form for the first time. Many of the missions gradually became very well established on the Gold Coast. But the aloof manner that some of the missionaries displayed toward the African peoples they had come to help often caused resentment among the local populations.

The Beginnings of British Rule

At first, British power and influence had been limited to the coastal forts and to ports used by British ships. British merchants were interested in protecting the settlements and furthering peaceful trade with the Africans. In time, however, the merchants found that they could not control all of the internal competition that their trading had created.

By the late eighteenth century, the Asante had organized themselves into a powerful military confederacy. Their aim was to expand their influence toward the coast. For the most part, this policy was motivated by economic concerns. The Asante territory was located inland, and European goods were obtainable in the interior only at very high prices. The coastal Africans—the Fante and Accras—served as go-betweens in the trade deals. The Asante wanted to conquer the coastal African peoples to establish direct links with European merchants.

Consequently, the Asante began continual raids on the coastal peoples. Protection of the settlements and of the coastal trade

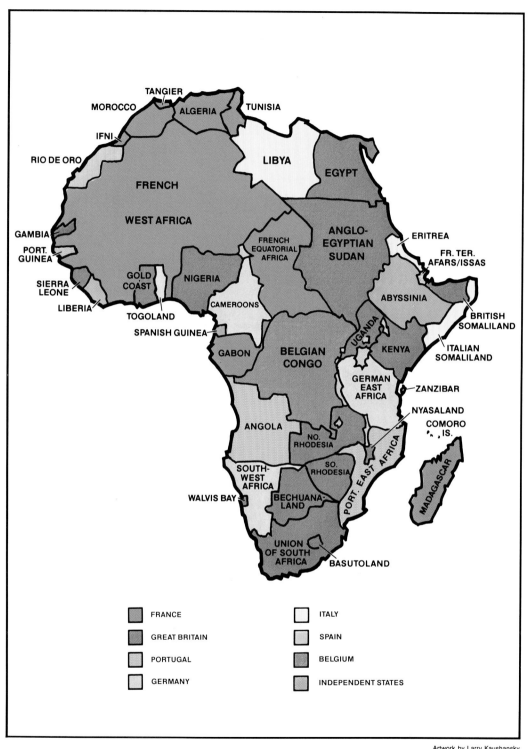

TANGIER

MOROCCO   ALGERIA   TUNISIA

IFNI

RIO DE ORO

FRENCH

WEST AFRICA   LIBYA   EGYPT

GAMBIA   FRENCH   ANGLO-   ERITREA
PORT.   EQUATORIAL   EGYPTIAN
GUINEA   AFRICA   SUDAN   FR. TER.
AFARS/ISSAS

GOLD   NIGERIA
COAST   ABYSSINIA
SIERRA
LEONE   CAMEROONS   BRITISH
LIBERIA   SOMALILAND
TOGOLAND
UGANDA   KENYA   ITALIAN
SPANISH GUINEA   SOMALILAND

GABON   BELGIAN
CONGO   GERMAN   ZANZIBAR
EAST
AFRICA   NYASALAND
ANGOLA   COMORO
NO.   IS.
RHODESIA
SOUTH-   SO.
WEST   RHODESIA   MADAGASCAR
AFRICA
WALVIS BAY   BECHUANA-
LAND   PORT. EAST AFRICA

UNION
OF SOUTH
AFRICA   BASUTOLAND

	FRANCE		ITALY
	GREAT BRITAIN		SPAIN
	PORTUGAL		BELGIUM
	GERMANY		INDEPENDENT STATES

Artwork by Larry Kaushansky

By the late nineteenth century, European powers had carved the continent of Africa into areas of influence. Present-day Ghana was included in the region called the Gold Coast that was claimed by Great Britain. Map information taken from *The Anchor Atlas of World History,* 1978.

became expensive for Britain. In 1828 the British government voted to dismantle the forts and to leave the territory entirely.

British merchants, however, were not eager to depart, and the coastal Africans were fearful of being left to face the Asante alone. The British government compromised by handing over the administration of their settlements to a committee of three London merchants. The settlements were to be administered under a governor and an elected council. This arrangement laid the foundations of British rule.

Colonization of the Gold Coast

While the British were trying to control their holdings in West Africa, other European powers were scrambling to establish colonial possessions throughout Africa. When the French and the Germans moved into areas of British trade, Britain decided to strengthen its claims and reestablished control of the Gold Coast. During the Berlin Conference of 1884–1885, European governments discussed the issue of whose influence was going to be recognized in which territory.

Within the Gold Coast region, treaties already existed between British merchants and coastal peoples, but the British governor was still concerned about the Asante. In 1896 British troops occupied Kumase, the capital city of the Asante lands, and declared the territory a protectorate of Great Britain. The Asante, however, continued to resist being included in the British colony. In 1900 another Asante-British war broke out, but this time the Asante were severely defeated. The same year, the Northern Territories—a region covering 30,600 square miles across the northern third of present-day Ghana— were also declared to be part of Britain's protectorate.

In the 1920s, after World War I, Britain was given one-third of the former German colony of Togoland. That acquisition completed the collection of lands that make up modern Ghana—the Gold Coast colony, the Asante region, the Northern Territories, and British Togoland.

Photo by Eliot Elisofon, Eliot Elisofon Archives, National Museum of African Art, Smithsonian Institution

An Asante court at Kumase holds a reception for a visiting northern leader, or chief. Unlike other Ghanaian ethnic groups, the Asante people continued to resist British intervention during the nineteenth century. The final Asante attempt—the Yaa Asantewa War of 1900—failed to drive the British from Ghana, however, and Ghana soon became a British colony.

The Early Twentieth Century

When the British took control of the combined territory in the early twentieth century, they established a centralized government. A governor directed the affairs of the country with the assistance of Executive and Legislative councils. The Executive Council—which up to 1943 consisted only of European officials—advised the governor. The Legislative Council voted on taxes and made laws. Both Africans and Europeans were represented in this body, but its members were appointed by the governor, not elected by the people.

The traditional local leaders and groups of African professionals were not satisfied with this system. As a result, two separate African protest movements developed. Established in 1897, the Aborigines' Rights Protection Society succeeded in increasing the power of the traditional leaders for stating local opinion. In the 1920s the National Congress of British West Africa—made up of African doctors and lawyers—at first opposed the advisory role of the local leaders. Later, however, the congress worked with local leaders in order to retain more control of the government.

The Post–World-War-II Era

After World War II, discontent over colonial conditions grew throughout Africa. Within the Gold Coast, a seminational political party—the United Gold Coast Convention (UGCC)—was formed in August 1947, under the leadership of Africans George Grant and J. B. Danquah. This group spoke against the government for failing to deal with the country's difficulties and eventually demanded self-rule. In December 1947 the UGCC appointed a young Gold Coast student, Kwame Nkrumah, to become its general secretary and to activate the plans of the party.

Tensions remained strong in the country for many months. High prices led to a boycott of European goods, and rioting and looting broke out in several major cities. Fearful that events were getting out of control, Britain appointed a royal committee, called the Watson Commission, to investigate the riots. Although colonial powers were reluctant to agree to independence for their overseas possessions, the commission recommended the granting of more self-government to the people of the Gold Coast. An all-African committee—the Coussey Commission—was appointed to determine how the recommendations of the Watson Commission might be put into effect.

The Rise of Kwame Nkrumah

Before the Coussey Commission finished its work, Kwame Nkrumah left the UGCC. In June 1949 he formed the Convention People's party (CPP), which demanded immediate self-government.

Born in 1909 and educated in mission schools, Kwame Nkrumah worked his way through Lincoln University and the University of Pennsylvania. Ghana's first prime minister and later its president, Nkrumah was the undisputed leader of the government until he was ousted in 1966. He died in exile in 1972.

Nkrumah was serving a prison sentence for promoting a strike when he was elected to the legislative council in 1951. The governor, Sir Charles Arden-Clarke, released Nkrumah from prison the next day, and he was carried by enthusiastic crowds to Christiansborg Castle (now Osu Castle), where he was asked to form the first government of African ministers.

Nkrumah—a talented political organizer—and his followers soon brought their political message of immediate independence to the towns and villages of Ghana. The party's ideas went out to everyone —farmers, fishermen, artisans, women, and the young—from the savanna country of the Northern Territories to the fishing villages of the coast. Unlike all earlier political organizations in the country, the CPP demonstrated that it could rally nationwide support for a party and its policies.

In January 1950, when immediate self-government did not result from the Coussey Commission's report, Nkrumah ordered his followers to go on a general strike—that is, everyone was to stop working. As a result, he and other CPP leaders were imprisoned.

Based on the recommendations of the Coussey Report, a general election was scheduled for February 1951, while Nkrumah was still in prison. His party decided to participate in the election, and Nkrumah himself was a candidate for a legislative seat. The CPP won 80 percent of the seats, and the imprisoned Nkrumah was elected.

The governor, Sir Charles Arden-Clarke, had no choice but to release Nkrumah, who took his position as leader of the new legislative assembly. A striped prison cap became a symbol of the struggle for independence. At the same time, speaking in favor of self-government became a legal political activity. Under the Constitution of 1954, Africans at last began running their own government, except in areas of foreign affairs, defense, and the police. After that, full independence became even more likely.

Toward Independence

From 1954 to 1957, the main cause of discontent in the country was no longer the conflict between its African leaders and the British government. Disagreements arose among various political rivals within the country itself, and the old ethnic hostilities among peoples of the Northern Territories, the Asante, and coastal groups again emerged.

The first Gold Coast colony elections were held in 1951. The Convention People's party (CPP), which Nkrumah established in 1949, won 34 of the 38 seats in the Legislative Council.

Ethnic and religious associations, such as the Muslim Association party and the Northern People's party, developed in the Northern Territories. In the Asante lands, the National Liberation Movement (NLM) was launched in September 1954. Its leaders were mostly founding members of the UGCC who refused to join Nkrumah's party. The NLM presented the strongest and most organized opposition to the CPP.

Ethnic groups and political parties debated whether the independent nation should have a federal government or a central government. The CPP opposed a federation—in which several regional divisions and a main, central authority would share power—as impractical. It claimed such a system would be too expensive for a country of less than five million inhabitants, and that the costs of running the four or five proposed divisions would cripple the new country's economy.

The political parties were unable to reach any agreement over this important constitutional issue, and violence erupted, especially in the Asante territory. In May 1956 the government of Prime Minister Kwame Nkrumah issued a proposal for

On March 6, 1957, Ghana achieved its independence from Great Britain. Nkrumah *(above)* read the newspaper clippings about Ghana's independence with elation. As the first West African colony to gain independence, Ghana made worldwide news and encouraged the independence movement in other colonies. Former West African colonies, such as Senegal, Nigeria, and Sierra Leone, achieved self-rule in the early 1960s.

Gold Coast independence and for changing the country's name to Ghana. Britain soon announced that it would agree to Ghana's independence.

This agreement, however, was conditional. Great Britain would grant independence to Ghana only after a general election had been held and after a motion for independence had been passed by a majority of the newly elected legislature. The general election resulted in another gigantic victory for the CPP. The opposition parties dropped their demand for a federal form of government and instead asked for agreement on the constitution, which would go into effect upon independence.

The independent nation of Ghana became a reality on March 6, 1957. A few days later the new country was admitted into the United Nations.

The New Republic

Kwame Nkrumah dominated the first nine years of the new republic's history. Working to develop Ghana's economy and to improve living conditions, Nkrumah proposed a philosophy that opposed external interference and promoted industrialization. He also became prominent in international affairs, and many people viewed Ghana as an example of an African nation that was successfully adjusting to its independent status.

Throughout the 1950s, Kwame Nkrumah had stressed the need for Africans to think in terms of Pan-Africanism—that is, the union of all African groups. He encouraged practical steps toward aiding other African states to become independent. Two principal organizations arose to work for these goals—the Conference of

Independent Picture Service

Nkrumah soon took the initiative in promoting the union of all African states, a concept known as Pan-Africanism. In April 1958 he convened a conference of independent African states.

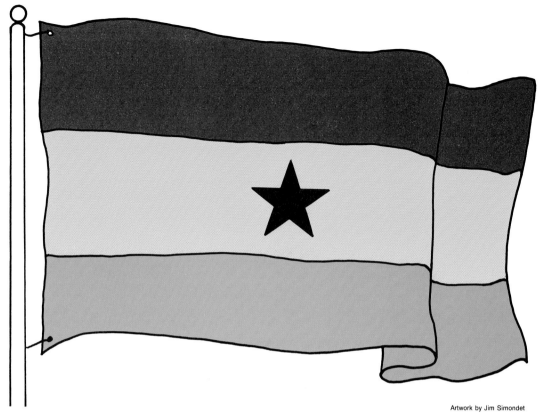

The colors of Ghana's flag have come to be known as Pan-African. Red symbolizes the revolution and the blood of those who fought for independence; yellow represents the country's natural resources (chiefly gold); and green stands for agricultural resources. The star is the symbol of African freedom.

Independent African States and the All-African Peoples' Conference. Ghana played the most important role in organizing both conferences.

Before long, however, it became clear that Nkrumah was neither as neutral nor as practical as he had declared. He increased his power, in part by eliminating all opposition parties, and became a virtual dictator. He borrowed huge sums of money from abroad to begin ambitious projects that the country could not afford. Instead of improving agricultural production and building industry, for instance, he authorized construction of the lavish Black Star Stadium in Accra. He also organized ideological groups to persuade young people to adopt his philosophy and needlessly increased the size of the government.

Because of these actions, internal opposition to Nkrumah began to build. People felt that their rights—guaranteed by the Constitution of 1960—were being violated. Moreover, some Ghanaians believed that the Nkrumah administration was keeping them in poverty while the government leaders were becoming wealthy.

Although Nkrumah and the CPP failed to bring prosperity to Ghana, they did achieve some worthwhile goals. In education and health, for example, Ghana had an impressive record by the 1960s. Tema Harbor, which was built during the Nkrumah administration, still handles the bulk of the country's shipping traffic. The Akosombo Dam, also a Nkrumah project, provided hydroelectric power to fuel Ghanaian industry.

Changing Leadership

The dissatisfaction with Nkrumah and his party finally resulted in a coup d'état on February 24, 1966. It was led by Colonel E. K. Kotoka, Police Inspector General J. W. K. Harlley, and A. A. Afrifa while Nkrumah was on a state visit to China. A group of eight military and police officers formed the National Liberation Council, which was headed by Lieutenant General J. A. Ankrah.

One of the first acts of the National Liberation Council was to assign the job of drawing up a new constitution to a legal

Courtesy of Ruth Karl

Black Star Square in Accra is one of many monuments to African unity and liberation constructed during Nkrumah's administration.

Ghanaian children gather around a fallen statue of Kwame Nkrumah in Accra in 1966. Although he came to power as a popular hero, Nkrumah soon transformed the government into a dictatorship, and his unwise spending led to economic chaos. In February 1966, while Nkrumah was visiting China, a group of army officers carried out a coup d'état against Nkrumah's regime.

Independent Picture Service

After the coup of 1966, eight military officers, who made up the National Liberation Council, assumed power in Ghana.

committee. The constitution went into effect in August 1969, after which the National Liberation Council was dissolved and Ghana returned to civilian rule and democratic procedures.

Unfortunately, the new administration—led by Kofi Busia and his Progress party—excluded the Ewe and other ethnic groups. Moreover, in order to balance the budget, the government cut off funds needed for social and economic improvements. Many Ghanaians opposed the regime because it was ethnically biased and designed to protect the interests of the rich.

As a result, in January 1972 an army officer named Ignatius K. Acheampong overthrew the democratic administration and established a second military regime. Acheampong's cabinet was more ethnically balanced but grew increasingly strict. His authoritarian rule came to an end as a group of senior officers demanded his resignation in 1978 and formed a third military government.

Before a civilian government could be elected, Lieutenant Jerry Rawlings intervened for four months, supported by young Ghanaians, by the poor, and by many people of the Ga and Ewe groups. A northerner, Hilla Limann, was elected president in late 1979. Limann's government, however, failed to win over many Ghanaians whose economic and political frustrations had been given a focus by Rawlings. Consequently, on New Year's Eve 1981, Rawlings again intervened to end Ghana's third unsuccessful experiment in civilian government, thus beginning the fifth military regime.

The Unstable Eighties

Ghana's economy—already in a downward spiral due to severe drought conditions in the late 1970s and early 1980s—suffered further setbacks for another reason. During the early 1980s, primarily in response to the nation's serious economic problems, a steady stream of Ghanaians, including many teachers and doctors, left Ghana to find work in Nigeria. But Nigeria also was experiencing economic troubles, and in 1983 its government forced about one million Ghanaians to return to Ghana. Their return worsened already high unemployment and created shortages of food, housing, and water.

The Rawlings administration—despite its attempts to heal the country's ailing economy—has often met with opposition. From 1981, when Rawlings seized power, until 1984, five known plots to topple the military government were attempted.

In 1985 and 1986, favorable amounts of rainfall enabled farmers to expand agricultural production, which improved the economy somewhat. Ghana became self-sufficient in palm oil, rice, yams, and cassavas. In addition, exports of cacao and timber increased slightly, and mining improved.

Nevertheless, the overall economic crisis in Ghana continued, and the nation was

Lieutenant Jerry Rawlings is the leader of Ghana's current military government, the Provisional National Defense Council (PNDC). Rawlings first established power in 1979 by a violent coup. His is the fifth regime in power in Ghana since Nkrumah's fall in 1966.

A policewoman directs traffic in Accra.

forced to seek a large loan from the International Monetary Fund, an agency of the United Nations. Thus, in 1986—with no lasting improvement in the unstable economy—worker discontent mounted. Many Ghanaian citizens protested the government's strictness in economic matters, and at least three more plots against Jerry Rawlings were uncovered.

Government

The Constitution of 1979 had provided for an executive president to be elected directly by Ghanaians. Since the coup d'état in 1981, however, the provisions of that constitution have been suspended. In its place, a military government has been organized, which consists of a 10-member Provisional National Defense Council (PNDC) headed by a special adviser. For administrative purposes, the nation is divided into 10 regions.

Governmental systems at the local level range from revived ethnic and village-based leadership to new political experiments that vary widely from one community to the next. Both traditional and newly created structures for resolving conflicts and

Courtesy of Dr. Deborah Pellow

Candidates from six political parties competed in the presidential race of 1979. A float led a rally held for the candidate of the United National Convention (UNC) party.

for administering justice have been explored. The forms of government that favored a small group of people before the revolution continue to exist at the national level. But rule by the few has been challenged by many who feel that such a system is no longer appropriate in Ghana.

Courtesy of Dr. Deborah Pellow

Students at the University of Ghana demonstrated in the streets of Accra in 1979. Conflict, unrest, and instability have characterized the last decade of Ghanaian politics.

A Hausa woman holds her grandchild. The Hausa, who originally migrated from Nigeria, inhabit northern Ghana and specialize in kola nut trading.

3) The People

With a population of 14.4 million people growing annually at a rate of 3.1 percent, the population of Ghana will double in 22 years. Half of all Ghanaians are under 18 years old.

Ethnically, Ghana's population is a melting pot that represents a wide variety of African, European, and Asian peoples. About 99 percent are black Africans, who belong to roughly 100 different ethnic groups. About one percent of Ghana's population is of Asian or European descent.

The Akan peoples—made up of the Asante, Fante, Akwapim, Brong, Akim, Nzima, and other smaller units—live in the south central and coastal regions. The Akans make up 44.1 percent of Ghana's population. Other important ethnic groups are the Mole-Dagbani and Hausa, who live in the north; the Ewe, who live in the southeast Volta Region; and the Ga-Adangme, who live near Accra. These groups have separate languages, and their customs and traditions are also unique.

Traditions and Culture

In the years since Ghana achieved independence, many important changes have taken place in the physical appearance of the country. For example, fine buildings have been constructed, new roads cross the country, and schools and hospitals have been built. Despite the convenience of these modern improvements, however, many Ghanaians believe a conscious effort must be made to preserve their cultural history.

For this reason the institution of the chieftaincy, or the rule of local leaders, and the ceremonies attached to it are kept alive today. Although these leaders no longer enjoy the status and power they once had, they see themselves as the protectors of Ghana's cultural heritage. The chieftains still oversee festivals, which are full of pomp and dignity and which draw participants from miles around.

Courtesy of Embassy of Ghana

At a durbar, or ceremonial gathering, the honored chieftain rides atop the shoulders of others in an enclosed seat called a palanquin.

The climax of a festival is generally a durbar—a great gathering of secondary local chieftains and their followers, who assemble to honor the highest ranking chieftain. Lasting about an hour and a half, the durbar begins with a formal procession through the town. The chieftains ride in palanquins (enclosed seats carried by poles on the shoulders of others), shaded from the sun by large, colorful umbrellas and surrounded with attendants. At the ceremonial grounds, greetings are exchanged and the state executioners—who are purely ceremonial officials—describe old battles. Following this event, the main chieftain addresses the people. Food and folk dancing end the festivities.

The establishment of museums, craft centers, and African studies courses offers another important means of saving Ghana's cultural history. Kumase's historical museums and the Manhyia Palace —former home of the Asante king Asantehene—preserve some of the rich heritage of the Asante people. Still the center of many Asante cultural activities, Kumase also houses the National Cultural Centre. Here, talented local artisans work at traditional Ghanaian crafts—designing *kente* and *adinkra* cloth, weaving, carving wood, and fashioning figures and weights made of brass, bronze, and clay.

Religion

Many Christian churches, Islamic mosques, and local religious shrines exist throughout Ghana. Almost half of Ghana's population, concentrated mostly in small villages, still practices traditional African beliefs and relies on local spiritual leaders. Christianity—which arrived with European and U.S. missionaries—has been adopted by approximately 40 percent of the people. About 12 percent are followers of Islam, which was introduced by Muslim traders from the north.

Most rural Ghanaians, as well as many people who live in the country's towns and

40

Simple looms are still used to weave silk and cotton threads into long strips for making kente cloth. The colorful, narrow strips are then hand-stitched together to form the full width of the traditional fabric.

Traditional crafts, such as brass sculpting (above) and pottery (right), are still popular in Ghana. Ghanaian culture continues to preserve strong ties to its past.

41

Drumming, dancing, and feasting highlight most Ghanaian festivals. Music and dance are combined with storytelling to celebrate a harvest or to commemorate a historical event. The performers' clothing often displays beads or other artwork designed by local craftspeople.

Courtesy of Mark Killen

cities, accept the view that all objects, persons, animals, and special places possess a natural life force or vitality. This view helps them to answer questions regarding the nature of the universe, the forces that control it, and the role of humans within it. Such beliefs have inspired a rich collection of folklore and folk art and have helped shape people's rules for behavior.

Music and Literature

The oldest and best-known object in Ghanaian traditional activities is the drum. It is used on social, military, and political occasions for talking, singing, and dancing. Drums are carved from the *kyendur* tree, and most are covered with the skin of a

black antelope. The *atumpan,* or talking drum, is covered with elephant skin.

The atumpan consists of a pair of drums that are so big they must be supported by props. Serving as Ghana's most important percussion instrument, the atumpan is used to transmit messages. On festival occasions, the atumpan "speaks" of the traits and achievements of kings and other individuals. Legend has it that clever drummers were able to persuade whole states to take up arms against one another.

Traditional Ghanaian dancing matches the artistry of ceremonial drumming. The dancers move swiftly with intricate steps and a strong sense of timing. Each movement in the dance conveys an idea or a message. Creative variations of the original dance patterns are often inspired by the multiple tones and rhythms of accompanying drums.

Ghanaian novelists, poets, and playwrights have made substantial contributions to world literature in the past 30 years. Most novelists focus on urban life, developing themes such as political and social corruption. One recurring subject stresses the harm caused when respected African values are influenced and distorted by contact with Western societies. Well-known works include Asare Konadu's *A Woman in Her Prime;* Kofi Awoonor's *This Earth, My Brother;* and Ayi Kwei Armah's *The Beautyful Ones Are Not Yet Born.*

The *atumpan,* or "talking drum," is used to tell stories or transmit messages.

Ghanaian dancing can be as expressive as language. Each subtle movement in a dance conveys a recognizable meaning, and various combinations of movements often tell parts of a message or story.

43

Education

Serving as both the official and the commercial language, English is taught in all Ghanaian schools. Nevertheless, only about 30 percent of the general population can read and write in English. Most Ghanaians, however, can speak English and at least one other of the 50 languages and dialects of the area. The most important African languages include Twi, Fante, Ga, Ewe, Hausa, and Dagbani.

The development of Ghana's educational system is part of many government projects. In addition, educational expansion is a primary goal among adults for their children, their families, and themselves. It is not uncommon in Ghana for a teacher to punish disobedient children by forbidding them to come to school for the next day or two. This form of punishment is recognized as the most severe penalty that a teacher can inflict.

Independent Picture Service

The government's Department of Social Welfare and Community Development teaches rural adults to read and write. In the 1980s studies indicated that 30 percent of Ghana's population was literate in the English language.

Independent Picture Service

Students of the Amedzofe Teacher Training College take notes on practical methods at an elementary school. The demand for instructors in Ghana has risen dramatically in the last decade.

A student takes time for more reading before graduation ceremonies at the University of Ghana.

Since 1973 public education in Ghana has been free—except for textbook fees—at all levels. Children must attend school until they are 12 years old.

Ghana has developed three universities since 1948: the University of Ghana at Legon, the Kumase University of Science and Technology, and the University College of Science Education at Cape Coast. The Institute of African Studies—which provides graduate studies in African sociology, history, anthropology, music, language, drama, dance, and art—is a part of the University of Ghana.

In addition to education in the regular school system, mass-education campaigns have brought literacy to thousands of adults in rural villages. This is largely the work of the government's Department of Social Welfare and Community Development. Teaching people to read and write is only part of the department's work. It also trains them in child care and village development, and it conducts campaigns to improve health, agriculture, and housing in the villages.

Despite overall expansion, however, Ghana's educational system has not kept pace with its population growth. There are not enough public schools; in addition, the continuity and quality of existing schools suffered recently when many teachers left Ghana for Nigeria. Improvements in staff, curriculum, and facilities are all needed, and many Ghanaians are beginning to speak out for assistance in gaining them.

Noted Ghanaian scholar L. H. Ofosu-Appiah has served as director and editor of the *Encyclopaedia Africana* since 1966. He also has translated Homer's *Odyssey* into Twi, a local language.

Health

Under Nkrumah, as well as under some regimes that followed, the government of Ghana attempted to take a strong position that promised inexpensive and comprehensive health care. Unfortunately, in the past 10 years a large number of doctors who were frustrated with the deteriorating quality of Ghanaian life left the country.

Life expectancy in Ghana increased from 44.8 years in 1960 to 58 years in 1988. The infant mortality rate—72 per 1,000 live births—is favorable compared to the average of 110 for all of Africa. Healthy diets, however, have been difficult to achieve in Ghana, especially since the severe droughts of the late 1970s and early 1980s. Because food sources continue to be unstable, many people do not eat the minimum requirements for adequate daily nutrition.

Disease remains a major health threat. About 30 percent of recorded deaths are from diseases that, with proper treatment,

A government health worker arrives with medicine to help combat malaria. As a follow-up in the campaign against disease-carrying mosquitoes, villagers are urged to spray their homes with insecticide frequently.

Courtesy of Professor Barbara Killen

A street vendor in Accra sells various items, such as eggs, tuna, soap, and aspirin—all of importance to the health of Ghanaians. In the late 1970s and early 1980s, however, government changes resulted in efforts to prevent traders from selling these practical commodities, and access to the goods became difficult.

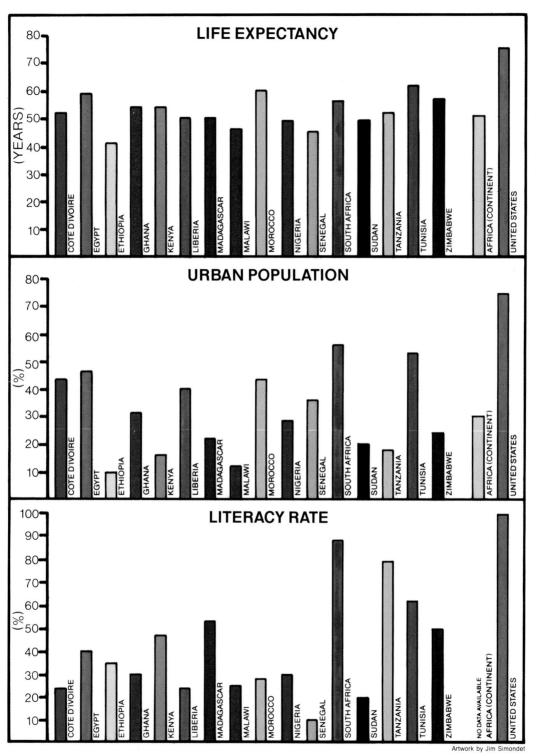

LIFE EXPECTANCY

(YEARS)

COTE D'IVOIRE · EGYPT · ETHIOPIA · GHANA · KENYA · LIBERIA · MADAGASCAR · MALAWI · MOROCCO · NIGERIA · SENEGAL · SOUTH AFRICA · SUDAN · TANZANIA · TUNISIA · ZIMBABWE · AFRICA (CONTINENT) · UNITED STATES

URBAN POPULATION

(%)

COTE D'IVOIRE · EGYPT · ETHIOPIA · GHANA · KENYA · LIBERIA · MADAGASCAR · MALAWI · MOROCCO · NIGERIA · SENEGAL · SOUTH AFRICA · SUDAN · TANZANIA · TUNISIA · ZIMBABWE · AFRICA (CONTINENT) · UNITED STATES

LITERACY RATE

(%)

COTE D'IVOIRE · EGYPT · ETHIOPIA · GHANA · KENYA · LIBERIA · MADAGASCAR · MALAWI · MOROCCO · NIGERIA · SENEGAL · SOUTH AFRICA · SUDAN · TANZANIA · TUNISIA · ZIMBABWE · NO DATA AVAILABLE AFRICA (CONTINENT) · UNITED STATES

Artwork by Jim Simondet

The three factors depicted in this graph suggest differences in the quality of life among 16 African nations. Averages for the United States and the entire continent of Africa are included for comparison. Data taken from "1987 World Population Data Sheet" and *PC-Globe.*

could easily be cured. These include malaria, tuberculosis, typhoid, sleeping sickness, leprosy, and river blindness.

The overall medical situation in Ghana is critical. Malnutrition is widespread—especially among immigrants in urban shantytowns with no garden plots. Ghanaians living in the northern areas are experiencing famine, due to drought conditions and disastrous bushfires that destroy field crops of plantains, yams, and cassavas. Enclosed drainage and sewage systems are inadequate throughout the country, and standing pools of dirty water breed malaria-carrying mosquitos. Water and fresh foods can be dangerous unless properly prepared.

The World Health Organization (WHO) is coordinating research, education, and treatment for AIDS—acquired immune deficiency syndrome. Insufficient health information and substandard medical facilities have contributed to the spread of this epidemic disease. By mid-1987 only 73

Courtesy of P. Almasy, World Health Organization

Running water is available mainly in urban areas. Access to clean water is an important health concern for Ghanaians.

Courtesy of UNICEF

An herbalist dispenses his unique remedy to a village woman. Except for the Western-educated urban population, most people in Ghana prefer the services of herbalists and healers to more modern medical treatments.

48

Ghanaian men often wear kente cloth draped over one shoulder in the manner of a Roman toga.

cases had been reported in Ghana, with 118 cases in neighboring Côte d'Ivoire and none in Burkina Faso or Togo. WHO suspects, however, that unreported cases of the disease may affect over two million people throughout the continent.

For many Ghanaians, local healers are the only medical help available. By 1979 traditional midwives, or *matrones*, had been trained in hygienic delivery by the government's Danfa Project. The matrones—who are trusted by the general population—deliver more than 75 percent of babies born. They also offer prenatal care and treat complications of pregnancy and delivery, thus helping to fill the country's need for medical personnel.

Clothes

Western-style suits and dresses are the everyday wear of people in Ghana's towns, but traditional, graceful kente cloth is often worn for formal, ceremonial, or evening occasions. Cotton kente cloths are handwoven on narrow looms. The strips are then sewn together by hand to make six or seven yards of material. The weaving of kente cloth is a very old and delicate art that dates back some 250 years. Each pattern tells a different story and represents a different history. Men drape kente cloth over themselves in the style of Roman togas. Women use the fabric to fashion full-length skirts, blouses, and matching wraparound garments.

Besides kente cloth—which is too expensive for most people to wear every day—brightly printed cotton fabrics are also worn. The patterns are designed by artists in Ghana, and the fabric is processed in Britain and Holland. Frequently the patterns pay tribute to a particular person or occasion.

Food

Staple foods in the Ghanaian diet include yams, cassavas, maize, plantains, and rice. Many fish dishes, as well as a variety of tropical fruits and vegetables, are also commonly eaten.

Traditional soups (such as palmnut and peanut) and stews (such as *kontomere,* okra, and spinach) are usually enjoyed with *fufu*, a starchy accompaniment. *Gari*, or toasted cassava flour, is the staple dish consumed by low-income groups. Since many Ghanaians enjoy hot and spicy food, a pepper sauce made with a base of meat, fish, or chicken is served with most meals.

Courtesy of UNICEF

Pepper *(above)*, an ingredient in nearly every recipe in Ghana, is ground by a young woman using the same technique and tools her great-grandmother used. *Fufu (below)*—a starchy dough made from mashed yams, cassavas, or plantains—remains a popular part of the Ghanaian diet.

Courtesy of Dr. Deborah Pellow

A woman carries yams, a staple food in Ghana, to sell in a market in Accra.

Courtesy of UNICEF

The exposure of young Ghanaians to soccer begins at an early age.

Sports

The people of Ghana are keen sports enthusiasts. Soccer—the national game, controlled by the Ghana Sports Council—is by far the most popular sport. Other athletic events include boxing, hockey, track and field, horse racing, table tennis, basketball, swimming, gymnastics, cricket, polo, squash, lawn tennis, judo, and cycling.

Many talented Ghanaians also participate in international competitions. Since 1952 Ghanaians have been active and successful participants in both Olympic and British Commonwealth events.

An ancient board game known as *oware* is also greatly enjoyed throughout the country. Played with palm nuts, dried beans, or pebbles, it demands lightning-quick mental arithmetic.

Soccer—called football in Ghana—is the national sport and enjoys tremendous popularity.

Courtesy of Dr. Deborah Pellow

Trading—generally informal, open-market commerce—is the largest occupational category in Ghana. Most of the traders are women.

4) The Economy

Despite the natural and skilled human resources available in Ghana, its economy has not been able to sustain any measure of growth in recent years. Budget deficits are common, and the foreign debt has skyrocketed. Demands for higher wages as well as shortages of imported consumer goods—which put pressure on prices—have fueled inflation.

The downward spiral of Ghana's economy has been influenced by the global economic environment, but many national factors have wasted the country's assets as well. Businesspersons, military leaders, government officials, and individuals have used Ghana's resources to gain personal wealth at the expense of the whole society.

Although about 60 percent of Ghanaians are employed in agriculture and 17 percent in industry, almost one-fourth of Ghana's people live in absolute poverty. In 1984 Ghana's earnings from exports totaled $566 million, but its costs for imports—mainly petroleum, food, industrial raw materials, and machinery—totaled $616 million. Nevertheless, Ghana remains a country with considerable economic promise. Its people—through agriculture, fishing, forestry, and mining—have the potential to supply the needs of the nation.

Industry is a fairly small sector of Ghana's economy. Since experiments in state-controlled businesses proved unsuccessful, most industrial complexes are privately owned.

Ghana broadened its manufacturing base with the financial help of the Kaiser Aluminum and Chemical Corporation of California, whose support helped to introduce new workers and products into Ghana's industrial sector.

Agriculture

The most important crop grown in Ghana is cacao—the basic ingredient of chocolate. The product represents over 70 percent of all the goods that Ghana sells abroad. Export of this crop has long sustained the country's wealth, but the rise and fall of cacao prices on the world market make it difficult to predict earnings. Most of the funds spent on development projects in Ghana have come from cacao profits.

Almost one-fourth of Ghana's population is directly involved in the production of cacao. There are two harvests each year, the primary one lasting from October to February. Although Asante is the chief growing area—producing about 36 percent of Ghana's output—cacao is grown in most other forested areas of the country as well.

Other cash crops for export include bananas, kola nuts, limes, coffee, copra (dried coconut meat that yields coconut oil), shea nuts, and palm kernels. Farmers are encouraged to broaden their agricultural production—mainly by adding sugarcane, rice, citrus fruits, and vegetables—to avoid importing food. The moist valleys in the north and south are well suited to rice production, and many large fields are now under cultivation.

Independent Picture Service

A farmer shows his children healthy pods on a cacao tree. Cacao, grown in the southern forest regions, is Ghana's largest and most important export.

Large-scale farming is unusual in Ghana, however, since agriculture is dominated by small landholders who own farms of five acres or less. The humid forest region of the southwest produces

Independent Picture Service

Farmers break open cacao pods and remove the beans. The beans then are covered with leaves and are allowed to ferment for several days.

After fermenting, cacao beans must dry in the sun for six to eight days. During this time they are raked and turned several times a day. Eventually the beans will be made into chocolate.

rubber and bananas; livestock and food crops are raised in the drier southeast. Cassavas, coconuts, maize, yams, and sorghum are also grown.

Two prolonged droughts—from 1976 to 1977 and from 1982 to 1984—drastically affected Ghana's agriculture, especially in the north. Subsistence farming of food crops, which many Ghanaians depend upon, became impossible. The resulting serious shortage of food led to widespread malnutrition.

Fishing

By the mid-twentieth century, Ghana's carved and brightly painted canoe fleets—although picturesque and artistic—had become outdated. As the population grew, Ghana's traditional fishing methods could not keep pace with domestic demand for fish. Since 1957, however, Ghana's fishing

Bananas, grown in the humid forest region of the southwest, are weighed before shipping.

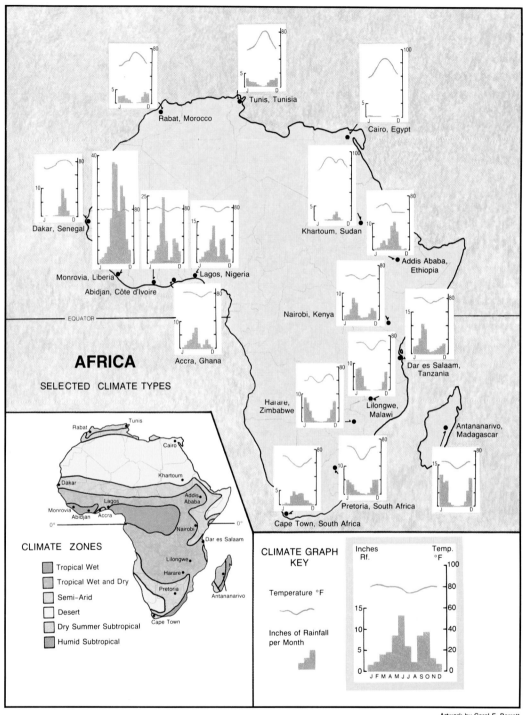

AFRICA

SELECTED CLIMATE TYPES

CLIMATE ZONES

- Tropical Wet
- Tropical Wet and Dry
- Semi-Arid
- Desert
- Dry Summer Subtropical
- Humid Subtropical

CLIMATE GRAPH KEY

Temperature °F

Inches of Rainfall per Month

Inches Rf.	Temp. °F

Artwork by Carol F. Barrett

These climate graphs show the monthly change in the average rainfall received and in the average temperature from January to December for the capital cities of 16 African nations. On the graph for Accra, Ghana, note that the capital is drier than the rest of the nation, which generally receives 40 to 80 inches of rainfall each year. Data taken from *World-Climates* by Willy Rudloff, Stuttgart, 1981.

equipment has expanded to include motorized canoes and modern boats with nets. Tema is the chief fishing port, followed by Elmina and Sekondi-Takoradi. Inland fisheries have also been developed on Lake Volta, where sardines, mackerel, and other fish are caught. An estimated 24,000 fishermen live with their families in the 920 fishing villages built along the shores of the lake.

Saltwater catches in the 1980s—including tuna, bream, and herring—averaged over 200,000 tons annually and satisfied 75 percent of the domestic demand. Ghana's ocean-fishing industry suffers, however, from poor marketing and a shortage of spare parts for the fishing fleet. Some U.S. companies located in Ghana have become involved in tuna fishing and canning.

Courtesy of OPIC

A fisherman brings in his catch of tuna. Fish are caught mainly for local consumption and provide Ghanaians with an important source of protein.

Photo by Phil Porter

The fishing industry in Ghana has grown rapidly since the 1960s, but some fishermen still use wooden canoes. About 85 percent of the annual catch comes from the ocean, while the rest is caught in inland rivers and lakes, especially in Lake Volta.

Because of the difficulties of transporting coastal fish to northern Ghana, fish farms were established in the upper northern regions. At first, these farms were highly productive, but since 1982 mismanagement and water problems have caused most of them to fail.

Forestry

Ghana's forests are rapidly diminishing, yet tropical hardwoods follow cacao as Ghana's second strongest export. Forestry operations generate about 10 percent of Ghana's foreign earnings. To help save this declining resource, the government occasionally controls cutting and marketing.

Most of Ghana's forestry output comes from areas located near the railway terminals—that is, near Sekondi-Takoradi,

Accra, and Kumase. Forest products are exported, however, only through Takoradi. Nearly 66 percent of these exports are logs—from wawa, utile, African mahogany, sapele, and makore trees. Efforts are being made, however, to increase the export of sawed lumber and plywood.

Sadly, failures in other areas of industry hinder the success of the timber business. For example, long-distance hauling by train has been inefficient, so logs lie rotting where they were felled.

Mining

The most important minerals mined and exported from Ghana are gold, diamonds, manganese, and bauxite (from which aluminum is made). Until about 1957, the mining industry—significant throughout

Courtesy of FAO

Ghana's large forest region supports a logging industry, which grew rapidly in the 1950s but which has since leveled off. After cacao, tropical hardwoods, such as obuke and wawa, make up the country's main export.

Miners extract gold, the precious metal for which Ghana became famous. The State Gold Mining Company, established in 1965, controls 35 percent of the industry. Gold production has declined in the last decade because of an unstable economy, transportation problems, old machinery, and smuggling.

The output of the mining industry has not increased in recent years, in part because no new mines have been opened since the 1930s.

Ghana's history—contributed more than one-fourth of the country's total exports.

This contribution has dropped to less than 15 percent for a number of reasons—world demand for some of the minerals declined, transportation is difficult, machinery is out-of-date, and smugglers have invaded part of the market. In addition, output in the mining industry has stayed the same or declined in recent years because no new mines have been opened. Equipment repair and management practices have deteriorated since the 1960s. Manganese, bauxite, and gold exports continue to decline, and the aluminum plant promised as part of Nkrumah's Volta River project has never been built.

Yet, in the 1980s, mineral exports ranked third after cacao and timber in terms of total export earnings. Ghana's richest gold mine is located at Obuasi, just south of Kumase, and diamonds come from the Birim area of the Eastern Region and from the Bonsa area of the Western Region. Ghana remains the world's second largest producer of industrial diamonds, although smuggling reduces the actual export value of this important industry.

Photo by Phil Porter

Construction of a dam to generate hydroelectric power was completed at Akosombo on the Volta River in 1966. Financial assistance for the project was provided by the United States, Great Britain, and the World Bank.

Volta River Project

The most daring of all the industrial schemes in Ghana is the extensive dam project on the Volta River. Previously, Ghana had to import diesel oil for supplies of electricity. The Volta River project, by producing cheap and plentiful hydroelectric power, has made Ghana less dependent on outside sources for its energy.

The huge dam and hydroelectric power station were completed in 1966 at Akosombo on the Volta. A principal consumer of Volta hydroelectricity in the early years was an aluminum refinery at the port of Tema. Although the project was originally intended to stimulate the development of Ghana's bauxite and aluminum resources, no new mines have been quarried. Energy now is transmitted to Accra, the capital city, and a separate ring of transmission lines about 400 miles long supplies power to towns, villages, and mines in southern Ghana.

Half of the $200-million project was financed by the Ghanaian government; the other half came from international loans, especially from the World Bank and the governments of the United States and Great Britain.

Unfortunately, since the mid-1980s the great outlay of money has had little positive impact on Ghana's economy. Lake Volta, however—stretching 325 miles above the Akosombo Dam—now provides inland transportation and is a potentially valuable resource for irrigation and fish farming.

Transportation

The expansion of Ghana's main road system is a top priority on the nation's list of development goals. In the mid-1960s Ghana boasted almost 20,000 miles of paved roads, which was a very impressive figure when compared with other African countries at the time.

Courtesy of Helaine K. Minkus

Paving Ghana's many dirt roads is a national priority.

Photo by Phil Porter

The ferry at Lake Volta is crowded with hundreds of passengers.

The Adomi Bridge, shown here under construction, was completed in 1957.

Ghana Airways, a state-owned corporation, offers limited service and is plagued by frequent breakdowns, overbooking, and mismanagement.

In addition, many bridges had been built, such as the Adomi Bridge over the Volta River, which was completed in 1957. One of the longest bridges in Africa, the 800-foot-long Adomi Bridge was a major step forward in linking two parts of the country previously connected only by ferry service.

Poor maintenance, however, has made many of Ghana's roads—including some of its major routes—barely passable in the 1980s. The lack of roads has, in turn, negatively affected the economy—especially by limiting the transport of food from the north.

Ghana's railroads—with almost 600 miles of rail—form a triangle connecting Accra, Sekondi-Takoradi, and Kumase. Deteriorating service has decreased passenger traffic, but the trains continue to haul manganese, bauxite, and timber to the coast for export.

Though once well served by international airlines, Accra's Kotoka International Airport has been functioning below capacity in recent years. Lufthansa, Pan American, and other foreign carriers have ceased operating in the country, and Ghana Airways offers poor service on domestic and foreign flights.

The Future

Once a creative and rich nation in West Africa, Ghana has gradually fallen into serious economic decline. Unemployment, inflation, poverty, and malnutrition are on the rise. Although the nation has the potential to become self-supporting in food production, mismanagement has prevented this achievement. Government bureaucracy drains almost two-thirds of the national budget.

The military regime of Lieutenant Jerry Rawlings faces a critical period during which it must respond to mounting discontent and despair. Some believe that continued and increased support from Western organizations is necessary for economic recovery. To prevent continued violent eruptions, a genuine forum must be provided for the dissent of intellectuals, students, and workers.

No single answer is clear for Ghana's political and economic recovery. An ineffective and inefficient civil service, however, must be replaced with honest, intelligent leadership. In addition, practical, technical knowledge is needed in order to increase Ghana's chances for success.

The future holds many questions for Ghana. Once Africa's model nation, Ghana now faces political and economic instability.

Courtesy of FAO

Index